DELICIOUS CHRISTMAS DECORATIONS

at Historic Houses and Your Home

by Patricia Hart McMillan

Schiffer Publishing Ltd

4880 Lower Valley Road • Atglen, PA • 19310

Printed in China

Other Schiffer Books By The Author:
Christmas at Historic Houses. Patricia Hart McMillan & Katharine Kaye McMillan, PhD. ISBN: 9780764335594. $45.00
Contemporary Villas. David Strahan, AIA, Katharine Kaye McMillan, Ph.D., & Patricia Hart McMillan. ISBN: 9780764337741. $59.99
Designing & Living with Glass Tiles. Patricia Hart McMillan, Liz Hart McMillan, & Katharine Kaye McMillan, PhD. ISBN: 9780764332661. $24.99
Glass Tile Inspirations for Kitchens and Baths. Patricia Hart McMillan & Katharine Kaye McMillan, PhD. ISBN: 0764325094. $19.95

Other Schiffer Books on Related Subjects:
Christmas Past. Robert Brenner. ISBN: 0764301721. $29.95
Snow Babies, Santas, and Elves: Collecting Christmas Bisque Figures. Mary Morrison. ISBN: 0887404936. $29.95

Library of Congress Control Number: 2011930063

Designed by Danielle D. Farmer
Cover Design by Bruce Waters
Type set in Algerian/Bernhard Modern BT/Dutch 809 BT

ISBN: 978-0-7643-3726-0
Printed in China

Schiffer Books are available at special discounts for bulk purchases for sales promotions or premiums. Special editions, including personalized covers, corporate imprints, and excerpts can be created in large quantities for special needs. For more information contact the publisher:

Published by Schiffer Publishing Ltd.
4880 Lower Valley Road
Atglen, PA 19310

Phone: (610) 593-1777; Fax: (610) 593-2002
E-mail: Info@schifferbooks.com

For the largest selection of fine reference books on this and related subjects, please visit our website at **www.schifferbooks.com**

We are always looking for people to write books on new and related subjects. If you have an idea for a book please contact us at the above address.

This book may be purchased from the publisher.
Include $5.00 for shipping.
Please try your bookstore first.
You may write for a free catalog.

In Europe, Schiffer books are distributed by
Bushwood Books
6 Marksbury Ave.
Kew Gardens
Surrey TW9 4JF England

Phone: 44 (0) 20 8392 8585; Fax: 44 (0) 20 8392 9876
E-mail: info@bushwoodbooks.co.uk
Website: www.bushwoodbooks.co.uk

Dedicated

to ten admirable friends who set beautiful tables:

Ann Sweet

Carolyn Slatton

Carole Old

Elizabeth Thompson

Lillian August

Lynda Hartsell

Louise Decker

Maryann Razzano

Norma Andrews

Olga Alexander Kenniburg Csar

Contents

PART ONE
INSPIRATION

Traditional Decorations at Historic Houses

It is easy enough to trace the craze for embellishing Christmas greenery with fruit to Colonial Williamsburg—source of so many decorating traditions that grow richer with each passing year.

According to an article by Libbey Oliver and Mary Theobald, in the Winter 1996-97 issue of the *Colonial Williamsburg Journal*, the legendary "Williamsburg Christmas look" began between 1936 and 1939, when Mrs. Louise Fisher was placed in charge of Christmas decorations. They report that Mrs. Fisher went to the Library of Congress looking for period examples to use as guides. Her "Della Robbia" fruit-and-greens wreaths—probably based on the carved wooden fruit-and-greenery swags by fifteenth century Italian sculptor Luca della Robbia—established the "Williamsburg Christmas look." To say "and the rest is history" is an understatement. Each year at Colonial Williamsburg, wreaths, swags, garlands, table runners, centerpieces, and bouquets of evergreens embellished with bright and beautiful fruit amaze, delight, and inspire!

Naturally decorative fruits with their gorgeous colors, characteristic shapes, and intriguing textures, can be seen in both grand homes (including the Governor's Palace in Colonial Williamsburg) and modest historic houses in Williamsburg and across the nation. These arrangements—for the most part not edible—offer exciting inspiration and real design direction.

In "Interpretation—Bringing Tradition Home," *page 47*, there are four arrangements inspired by historic house museums and our interpretations, using real fruit with real or in some cases *faux* greenery. They demonstrate how easy it is to follow the examples of historic house designers.

NOTE: *Creating even one decoration may be the beginning of a fun family tradition!*

Those who prefer to craft reproduction or to create their own interpretive designs in long-lasting dried-and-preserved fruit will find a source (Save-On-Crafts) in "Interpretation." Those who wish to work with "everlasting" *faux* fruit and greenery can find items in the annual Colonial Williamsburg Christmas catalog and on-line that make crafting easy. For the time-challenged, there are "ready-made" decorations. We show you decorations by Winward, a Colonial Williamsburg licensee. And there are beautiful items from NDI, available in retail shops and on-line.

Nothing quite matches the experience of seeing imaginative fruit-and-greenery decorations in their natural habitats—historic houses. But, while visiting in person should always be a high priority, the beautiful photographs in *Delicious Christmas Decorations* capture much of the magic of Christmas that begins at curbside and continues all through the house. We hope these images will inspire.

Curb appeal

Decorating the home for Christmas starts on the exterior. Here wreaths, garlands, and swags highlighted with brightly colored fruits decorate windows and entry doors. These colorful decorations create an exciting holiday vision for passersby and a warm welcome for holiday visitors. Likely in the past, some homeowners used real fruit on exterior decorations. Some historians doubt that the practice was widespread, because of rapid deterioration of the fruit, especially in certain climates, and the danger of attracting pests in all climates. Despite those two practical objections, the look is beautiful. Today real-looking *faux* fruit make it a breeze to get the look—with no fear that artful replicas will deteriorate or attract pests.

All through the house

Indoors there is hardly a surface that doesn't look more wonderful with a fruit-and-greenery decoration. Wreaths, garlands, and swags of fragrant greenery embellished with beautiful fruit adorn windows, doorways, stair railings, mantels, tabletops, and sometimes ceilings.

Even a formally draped dining table may wear a lavish, fruit-embellished swag of holiday greenery. Dripless dried and preserved fruits lend themselves beautifully to these decorations and as ornaments for the Christmas tree. Dried fruits preserve some of the unique colors and textures of fresh fruit, but do not deteriorate quickly. Some items, if stored properly, last more than one season. (See "Interpretations," *page 47*.) We provide a source for dried fruits (Save-On-Crafts) and we tell how to dry your own apples, oranges, and other fruits, should you so desire.

Historically, only fresh fruit was available to early Americans. And it was considered a luxury. In even the most luxurious historic homes, colorful fruit was often simply displayed in handsome bowls—first to be admired, then on a practical note, eaten. In historic houses across the country, bowls full of affordable and readily available bright red or green apples add interest to consoles and tables in hallways, living rooms, dining rooms, and kitchens. This simple decorating idea is easy to copy at home, where replenishing a bowl is not problem.

Many historic houses avoid the problems of real apples and pile real-looking everlasting *faux* fruit into handsome containers—to the surprise of the unsuspecting who take a bite! Adding glitter to *faux* fruit in houses of Victorians who loved the glamour tips the would-be taster to look, perhaps touch, but definitely not taste!

Clove-studded oranges go with every china style, including blue-and-white Chinese export ware and this Haviland Limoges porcelain coffee service. *Design by Patricia Hart McMillan, photograph by Barbara Justice.*

Bowls of oranges—a luxury to many in early times—were another favorite way to decorate a tabletop or mantel during the holidays. In homes of the affluent, oranges were often studded with whole cloves. The cloves added interesting contrasting color, pattern, and texture, turning already decorative oranges into captivating works of art.

Studding oranges with cloves is one decorating idea that appeals on several levels. For, not only do cloves add pattern to oranges, they add a delicious fragrance that wafts throughout the house. The aroma is a delight and welcome in all rooms, even on a bedside table. This idea may appeal to both grown ups and young people. Designing a pattern for the cloves adds a creative challenge that's fun, and pressing the clove stem into the orange rind is easy enough that children can help.

Arrangements in historic houses show that combining a variety of fruit results in more elaborate and fanciful arrangements. These can be seen in historic homes where budgets allowed and fruits were available. In these decorative arrangements, mixing fruits with contrasting colors, shapes, and textures creates great visual excitement. Greenery provides strong color contrast, and draped over the edges of containers, adds grace. Then, of course, greenery came from the garden. So decorations in the north tended to use fir, balsam, holly, or other evergreen trees. In the South, magnolia leaves were used. The idea then and now is to use what is handy.

Rich crystal and silver containers add elegance to fruit-and-greenery centerpieces for large, formal dining tables. Elevating gorgeous fruit arrangements on footed silver or glass containers or elegant stemware gives more importance. This is true of even a small arrangement meant for a console, desktop, or dresser. Decorative bowls—popular blue-and-white china, hand-carved rustic wooden bowls, silver, and crystal—are among the many, appropriate container choices seen in historic houses.

Multiplying the number of arrangements makes an even greater, more opulent statement—particularly on a very long formal dining table. In this case, an elaborate centerpiece, flanked by tall candlesticks or candelabra fitted with elegant tapers, is supported on each side by somewhat smaller, less grand but equally beautiful arrangements. On a console, a pair of decorative arrangements may flank an elegant wall-hung mirror or ancestor portrait. On a long buffet or sideboard, a large centerpiece may be flanked by secondary arrangements, and all three be united by a fruit-decorated garland stretched across the surface. The ideas and examples seem endless.

The Victorians—to whom too much never seemed quite enough—gussied up fruit-and-greenery arrangements by adding sparkling glass Christmas ornaments, beads, ribbons, and flowers. These elements contributed rich color, contrasting texture, and interesting pattern, all of which added glorious glamour to the naturally beautiful fruit. To further gild the lily, so to speak, fruits were glazed with crystallized sugar so that they glistened in the candlelight. This glazing became another favorite decorating art. Today, glitter, which is not inexpensive and definitely not edible, adds pizzazz to *faux* fruit *(see page 66)*. Save-On-Crafts sells high-quality German-made crystal on-line (see Sources)

A glazed pear accents a place setting at Hearthside Homestead. *Photography by Kathryn Hartley: courtesy Hearthside Homestead.*

Entries

Tropical fruits add bright color above the door and intriguing form and color to the holiday wreath hanging on the elegant door of the Joseph Webb House. The Webb House is one of three neighboring houses that comprise the Webb-Deane-Stevens Museum in Weathersfield, Connecticut. *Photograph by Charles T. Lyle, courtesy Webb-Deane-Stevens Museum.*

Entry doors, a key part of "curb appeal," create that important "first impression." Wreaths, garlands, and swags tell visitors that no matter the style or mood—formal or rustic, vivacious or well-mannered—inside all is merry and bright.

Let fruitful holiday decoration begin at curbside. Milliners Doris Warren and Brooks Wellborn hang a fruit-bedecked wreath on the railing at the Margaret Hunter Shop in Colonial Williamsburg. *Photograph courtesy The Colonial Williamsburg Foundation*

Lemons add a note of sunny yellow to a green wreath on the door of the Stevens House in Weathersfield, Connecticut. Historically, the lemons would have been real. Today, some historic houses use real-looking, long-lasting *faux* fruit. *Photograph by Charles T. Lyle, courtesy Webb-Deane-Stevens Museum.*

Red Delicious and green Granny Smith apples contrast vividly with a decorative, most imaginative strand of peanut shells in a unique wreath on the door at the Scriveners in Williamsburg, Virginia. *Photograph courtesy The Colonial Williamsburg Foundation.*

Christmas door plaques create a wreath effect on the door of the Coke-Garrett House. *Photograph courtesy The Colonial Williamsburg Foundation.*

A small wreath adds interest without blocking the view from the window. *Photograph courtesy Sherwood-Davidson House.*

Pineapples, the Colonial symbol of welcome, adorn a wreath on a door at the Coke-Garrett House. Apples add color. Shells and dried plants add local touches. *Photograph courtesy The Colonial Williamsburg Foundation*.

Consoles

Tops of consoles, dressers, chests, sofa/library tables, and desks are ideal places for decorations that add a lively, colorful note. Bowls of fresh, edible fruit are always welcome. Tuck in a few sprigs of greenery—perhaps savory herbs or holly with berries—for accent.

Classic Colonial arrangements of a pineapple surrounded by fruit—lemons in this case—enhance the tops of elegant consoles in the Joseph Webb House. *Photograph by Charles T. Lyle, courtesy Webb-Deane-Stevens Museum.*

Twin pyramid arrangements of lemons and greenery flank an elegant Chinese export porcelain punch bowl, one piece from the priceless Tudor Place ceramics collection from many countries. The collection spans over 200 years of ceramic art. *Photograph by Heather Bartlow, courtesy Tudor Place.*

A simple bowl filled with lemons, limes, and greenery contrasts vibrantly with a black console at Bidwell House in the Massachusetts Berkshires. *Photograph by Joanna Jennings, Staff, Bidwell House Museum.*

During the holidays, decoration can be just a bowl of cherries—actually a bright red cherry ball on a bed of greenery atop an elegant stemmed container. This one adds warm color to a tabletop at the Sherwood-Davidson mansion in Newark, Ohio. P*hotographs of the house by Bobbi Meldahl, Ryan Meldahl, and Emily Larson, courtesy The Sherwood-Davidson House.*

At the chic Campbell House in St. Louis, Missouri, host to President and Mrs. Grant and other luminaries of its day, bright oranges join pinecones and shining ornaments to create an exciting wreath. It hangs against an elegant mirror and calls attention to the bronze statue of Mercury. *Photograph courtesy Campbell House Museum.*

Mantels

Some interior designers declare that the hearth is the one piece of "furniture" that is vital to every room. A natural focal point, the fireplace provides physical and emotional comfort. No wonder that mantels are decorated to a fare-thee-well for the Christmas holidays. Mantels in historic houses may be elegantly formal, like those at Mount Clare, or playfully informal, incorporating children's toys, like the mantel at Campbell House in Saint Louis. All of these mantels are decorated, many with fruit and greenery.

Carla Murray at Maymont says that the massive oak mantel, heavily carved in the late nineteenth century revival of British or Northern European style, was meant to give a baronial hall effect to the Living Hall. Its opulence is underscored with elaborate fruit-flower-and-greenery swags and decorations for the Christmas holiday season. *Photograph by Gary Crallé, courtesy Maymont Mansion.*

Even when memory becomes blurred, details like a festive garland of greenery highlighted by bright oranges, grapes, and berries backed by antique Christmas cards remain clear. *Photograph courtesy Campbell House Museum, St. Louis.*

Glittering fruit, ribbon, doodads, and gewgaws—typically Victorian with its emphasis on finery—create dazzling excitement as mantel decoration at the Bingham-Waggoner home. *Photograph by Janeen Aggen, courtesy Independence, Missouri Tourism.*

Grapefruit and oranges—fresh from the groves and unretouched with dyes and paints—mix with shells and greenery on the simple mantel at the "cracker box" style house of award-winning author Marjorie Kinnan Rawlings. The arrangements reflect her gift for addressing matters of the heart genuinely and simply as she did in *The Yearling* and other novels. *Photograph by Kathleen Carr, courtesy Florida State Parks.*

In the study at Mount Clare, a graceful garland of greenery embellished with cheerful red fruit is draped asymmetrically across the mantel. Mounding fruit beneath the centered portrait creates a focal point that both balances and calls attention to the gilt clock depicting George Washington. The clock was made in 1805, by Dubue of Paris, France. *Photograph courtesy Mount Clare Museum House.*

The gracious Campbells entertained family, friends, and staff during the holiday season at their elegant home in St. Louis. Mantels were adorned with beautiful garlands of greens, highlighted by a medley of naturally colorful fruits. Interspersed candlesticks and art objects add interest. Over the mantel, a wreath sports bright-orange oranges. *Photograph courtesy Campbell House Museum.*

Lace doilies underscore the Victorian fruit and greenery garland in the dining room at Hearthside Homestead. *Photography by Kathryn Hartley: courtesy Hearthside Homestead.*

Brightly colored Oriental fans are bold backdrops for a fruit and greenery garland that graces a bedroom mantel at Bartow-Pell Mansion on New York's Long Island Sound. *Photograph by Tanya and Amanda Kraemer, courtesy Bartow-Pell Mansion Museum.*

Bedrooms

Fruits fancifully scored, clove-studded, and artfully decorated with ribbon fill a porcelain bowl, lending aromatic fragrance to a holiday bedroom.
Photograph by Patricia Schley, courtesy David Davis Mansion.

Appeal to the sense of smell with decorative arrangements of clove-studded oranges to brighten bedroom dressers and nightstands. Accent them with cinnamon sticks, or sprigs of Rosemary or eucalyptus.

At Riversdale, fruit, greens, and berries surround a cone (nowadays, it could be plastic or iron), creating an intriguing elevated base for the traditional pineapple. The arrangement, highlighted by a glowing candle—another symbol of welcome—adorning a windowsill is as suitable for a bedroom window as one in kitchen or parlor. *Photograph by Cassi Hayden, courtesy Riversdale House Museum.*

Dining Rooms

Repeating a color—in this instance orange—adds impact and need not be expensive. Here, vivid oranges add a colorful note to decorative wreaths and to fruit-and-greenery arrangements on table and mantel tops at Campbell House in St. Louis, Missouri. *Photograph courtesy Campbell House Museum.*

Dining room tables and buffets are second only to mantels when it comes to show-stopping arrangements. The more elaborate, the better, it seems. Don't be stingy when it comes to decorating a long table. This is the place for multiple arrangements united with garlands of greenery, ribbons, or strings of colorful beads.

A medley of fresh fruit forms the eye-catching centerpiece, while a beautiful red pear adds a decorative note to each place setting at the festive holiday table at Chinqua Penn. *Photograph by Amy Huber, courtesy Chinqua Penn Plantation.*

The dining room at the historic home of Barrister Charles Carroll is a treasure trove of antique porcelain and silver. An artful arrangement of fruit calls attention to the magnificent silver epergne centerpiece that was made in London in 1763. In the foreground, porcelain plates hold more brightly colored fruit. Also on the table and mantel are Nanking blue-and-white porcelain custard cups with tops. *Photograph courtesy Mount Clare Museum House.*

Orange tree branches with oranges intact mix with tropical flowers in a tall vase on the breakfast table at Whitehall, the Palm Beach home of Henry and Mary Lily Flagler. The Flaglers enjoyed breakfast at a set time daily in the Breakfast Room. Guests who were late ate in the nearby hotel! *Photograph courtesy Flagler Museum.*

In the "more is better" Victorian style, a fancifully beaded, frosted, iced, carved, beribboned, and bejeweled fruit-based concoction exuberantly graces the table at Hearthside, a house built as a grand romantic gesture to unrequited love. The mantel underscores the fruit-and-greenery plus theme. *Photograph by Ruth A.B. Clegg/Angell Fine Arts Ltd., courtesy Hearthside Homestead.*

At noon on December 7, 1912, seasonal red ribbons would have hung from the chandeliers, creating a canopy for the extravagant fruit centerpieces and reaching to the four corners of the beautifully dressed dining table at Maymont. The Dooleys, owners of Maymont, were hosting a luncheon for Governors and their wives from all of the United States of America. *Photograph by Katherine Wetzel, courtesy Maymont Foundation.*

For long tables, like this one at the Bingham-Waggoner House, a tall and beautiful footed glass or silver bowl filled with gorgeous fruit and embellishments is often flanked by matching or similarly styled containers of fruit. The fruit bowls can set on a beautiful runner, or be connected with trailing greenery or ribbons. *Photographs by Janeen Aggen, courtesy Independence, Missouri Tourism.*

The Governor's Palace was the epicenter of the social scene in early Williamsburg. In the dining room, the pineapple, a symbol of welcome, surrounded by beautiful (and costly) fresh fruit served as an elegant (and edible) centerpiece. This arrangement became a classic design. *Photograph courtesy The Colonial Williamsburg Foundation.*

The Colonial Williamsburg's Governor's Palace centerpiece design was eventually seen not just in dining rooms, but in rooms throughout houses across the country. Here, it graces a holiday table at the Sherwood-Davidson House in Newark, Ohio. *Photographs of the House by Bobbi Meldahl, Ryan Meldahl, and Emily Larson, courtesy The Sherwood-Davidson House.*

Fortunately for the thirsty, centerpieces need not be dry! Floating clove-studded oranges add color, pattern, and flavor to the traditional wassail bowl at the Crocker House in Michigan. *Photograph by Marcia Swiderski, courtesy the Crocker House Museum.*

Fruit, historically more available during the holiday season than cut flowers, was a natural and beautiful choice for a holiday centerpiece. Creative designs mix fruit and variegated greenery. Here, the arrangement in a footed crystal bowl is placed atop a mirror, making it even more glamorous. Silver candlesticks embellished with greenery and cranberry red candles add emphasis to the dining room of the David Davis family, friends and political allies of President Abraham Lincoln. *Photograph by Ken Kashian, courtesy David Davis Mansion.*

In the dining room of Campbell House in St. Louis—scene of festive meals for Presidents and Indian Chiefs—the buffet holds a lavish display of fruit and greenery. The focal point is an intricate arrangement of various fruits under a glass dome. Flanking the glass dome (and the brilliant mirror) are twin fruit-filled footed crystal bowls on elevated brackets that are integral to the exuberantly carved mirror frame. The three key elements—dome and bowls—are united by garlands of embellished greenery. The idea is simple, the effect stunning. *Photograph courtesy Campbell House Museum.*

Buffets—natural focal points for formal dining rooms—lend themselves to dramatic gestures. At Hearthside, twin topiaries beautifully decorated with Christmas ornaments flank fruit in a large footed hurricane-globe-shaped vase. Orange and amber color in fruits, ornaments, and the ribbon swag above unite these three glamorous pieces. *Photograph by Ruth A.B. Clegg/Angell Fine Arts Ltd., courtesy Hearthside Homestead.*

Pineapple centerpieces are at home all through the house during the holiday season. They are formal enough for the dining room and friendly enough for a console, family room, or kitchen. No glue-gun or elaborate preparations are necessary. Just elevate the pineapple (on something as simple as a small upturned bowl) and surround it with greenery and assorted fruit. *Photograph by Kathleen C. Ruse, courtesy Joel Lane Museum House.*

Fruit and greenery mix with other ornamental materials in a fanciful centerpiece on the long dining table. *Photography by Kathryn Hartley: courtesy Hearthside Homestead.*

Kitchens

The kitchen—never more important than in today's open floor plan homes—deserves holiday decorations. Fruit, with or without greenery, is a natural for table, countertop, and island!

A simple, hand-carved wooden bowl filled with unembellished fruit brightens the rustic kitchen table at Mount Clare. To follow the example, just wash and dry fruit thoroughly—and be prepared to refill the bowl often! *Photograph courtesy Mount Clare Museum House.*

A pineapple centerpiece, similar to those that decorated the Governor's Palace in Colonial Williamsburg, is ready in the kitchen for transport to the Mount Clare formal dining table. In this case, the symbolic pineapple is surrounded by bright red apples and vivid greenery, traditional Christmas colors. *Photograph courtesy Mount Clare Museum House.*

Fruit in a beautiful container is in the best of taste—pretty to look at and delightful to eat. In the Joel Lane House, bright oranges and greenery add color to an all-white filigree porcelain bowl. *Photograph by Kathleen C. Ruse, courtesy Joel Lane Museum House.*

PART TWO
INTERPRETATION

Bringing Tradition Home

Imaginative decorations at Historic Houses are thrilling. Once inspired to carry on the delightful tradition of decorating with fruit and greenery, we can choose to faithfully reproduce or loosely interpret a design, using real fresh fruit, dried-and-preserved real fruit, or *faux* fruit. We may also decide whether to use our decoration in a place similar to that of the historic house (mantel, console) or some other spot in our home.

DIY
Real Fruit Decorations—Four Interpretations

Here are four easy do it yourself (DIY) interpretations of decorations inspired by historic houses seen earlier in this book.

1. Sherwood-Davidson Mansion's Ball of Cherries

Inspiration

A red cherry ball adds a surprise note. *Photograph courtesy Sherwood-Davidson House.*

A red cherry (or cherry tomato) ball is both pretty and practical. *Styling by Patricia Hart McMillan, photograph by Barbara Justice. Opposite: Styling by Patricia Hart McMillan, photograph by Barbara Justice.*

Slender silver stemware holds a colorful ball of bright red cherries that decorates a surface at the historic Sherwood Davidson Mansion. This arrangement is easily copied for a cocktail or dining table by covering a grapefruit (or a Styrofoam ball) with cherries held on with colorful toothpicks. Greenery here is from an evergreen tree in a Texas garden. The silver "stemware" pairs a goblet and wine coaster from the Salvation Army. If guests are to pluck a cherry for eating, be sure and secure the coaster to the goblet. Use a grapefruit as the base and do not press the toothpick too far in but leave enough to grasp.

Tip: Tomatoes are fruit, so you could substitute cherry tomatoes! And although olives are not fruit—you could take the idea one step further and substitute olives—especially green olives stuffed with red pimento—great for a cocktail party.

2. Joel Lane House orange bowl

Tuck a few sprigs of herbs or evergreens in a bowl of fruit—what could be easier? *Photograph by Kathleen C. Ruse, courtesy Joel Lane Museum House.*

A small amount of colorful fruit is enough to add seasonal color. Placing a plate or platter under a small container makes the arrangement look more important. *Design by Patricia Hart McMillan, photograph by Barbara Justice.*

At the Joel Lane Historic House Museum, a blue-and-white porcelain bowl holds clove-studded oranges. Blue-and-white dinnerware, which grows more popular every year with magazine articles and books devoted to this beautiful china, is *everywhere*. In Texas, blue-and-white Haviland porcelain dinnerware is at home (not on the range) but on a seventeenth century refectory table *cum* buffet server. Only five clove-studded oranges are needed to make a large statement in a small bowl. The platter beneath it adds emphasis. Time needed to stud the oranges—about thirty minutes while watching a favorite TV program.

3. Lemons a la Tudor Place and Campbell House

A glass globe adds glamour and protection. *Photograph courtesy Campbell House Museum.*

Twin arrangements create classic symmetry. *Photograph by Heather Bartlow, courtesy Tudor Place.*

Pinecones contrast in color and texture with lemons in glass hurricane globes. Add pinecones to flanking lemon arrangements for unity. *Design by Patricia Hart McMillan, photograph by Barbara Justice.*

Lemons are yellow—the most visible color in the spectrum and a substitute touch of sunlight for gray wintry days. They're also oval and about the same size as the elegant egg, so they're easy to work into decorations. At the Campbell House in St. Louis, a designer combines them with other colorful fruit, then places the intricate design beneath a glamorous glass dome. At Tudor Place in Washington, D.C., lemons and sprigs of greenery cover a rounded cone. It is a very small creative leap to simply stack real lemons in glass hurricane globes (these are from Goodwill) to flank a decorative pinecone-filled bowl. They last for some time, and remain edible!

4. An elegant mantel, Mount Clare style

Asymmetrical arrangements can work beautifully with period furnishings. *Photograph courtesy Mount Clare Museum Home.*

Imitation—the sincerest form of flattery—makes decorating the mantel joyfully easy. *Design by Patricia Hart McMillan, photograph by Barbara Justice.*

At historic Mount Clare, an antique clock graces an elegant mantel treated to a lacy evergreen swag adroitly highlighted with colorful fruit, berries, and leaves. The look-alike mantel substitutes a candle-burning amber glass lantern from Marshal, a national retail chain that some decorators consider their secret source. *A faux* greenery swag augmented with sprigs of lacy, aromatic Rosemary from the garden, fresh Granny Smith apples, *faux* red berries, and *faux* orchids complete the decoration. The copy, while not as regal, is royally satisfying and gratefully does homage to Mount Clare.

DIY
Dried-and-Preserved Fruit Arrangements

Designing with dried fruit is made much easier by companies such as Save-On-Crafts, which makes a variety of fruits available online. Substitute them for real or faux fruits in decorations that replicate those in historic houses. There are whole oranges (orange and green-colored), decoratively slit then dried. Orange slices with rinds intact are translucent, turning light that passes through into a beautiful amber color that creates a mystical effect. Although we don't show examples, these slices are especially beautiful hung on a Christmas tree. A homeowner in Florida covered a 12-foot tall tree with dried orange slices and amber-colored lights. The effect was magical. Pile slices in a crystal container, accent with cinnamon sticks, and place the arrangement beneath a softly lit lamp on an end table. Place slices in a row along a swag lit with mini lights to grace a mantel. Pomegranates and pear gourds that look like pears offer options you are likely to see in historic houses during the Christmas holidays.

Dried orange slices are fascinating in arrangements or hung from Christmas tree branches. *Photograph courtesy Save-On-Crafts.*

Dried gourds that look like pears, artfully slit oranges, and rich-red pomegranates are only a few of the natural items that work in holiday decorations. *Photographs courtesy Save-On-Crafts.*

How To Dry Fruit

It is possible to dry your own fruit, including oranges, apples, pears, limes, and grapefruit. The process is fairly simple.

Step 1 – Cut the fruit into 1/8- to 1/4-inch-thick slices.
Step 2 – Preheat the oven to 200 degrees F.
Step 3 – Lay fruit slices on cooling rack, leaving space between pieces. Place the rack on a cookie sheet and the cookie sheet in the oven. Bake at 150 degrees F. for about 2 hours; then, turn slices over and bake for another 2 hours.
Step 4 – Remove the tray from the oven and let the fruit cool thoroughly to room temperature.

In an airtight container, store the cooled fruit in single layers (with space around each piece) separated by waxed paper to prevent their touching. To hang on a Christmas tree, use florist's wire, which a ribbon can easily cover.

Caution: Dried fruit used as decoration is no longer edible. This is especially true of fruit that is commercially dried and preserved for use specifically as decoration.

DIY
Faux Fruit Decorations

A piece of fruit centered on a white plate is color-coordinated with the border. *Photography by Kathryn Hartley: courtesy Hearthside Homestead.*

Beautiful individual faux fruits and greenery, together with forms that hold fruit in position, help the "DIYer" to create wonderful decorations that can be used again and again—adding to the sense of family tradition.

To see wonderful examples, go on-line to Williamsburg Marketplace at www.williamsburgmarketplace.com.

Hooray for Readymades

Centerpieces like the one seen at the David Davis Mansion inspire, but not everyone has time or perhaps the skill to make their own. Fortunately, Winward International is licensed by Colonial Williamsburg to create wonderful historically-inspired "everlasting" decorations that simplify decorating for the Holidays. Here are some. See others at www.WinwardSilks.com readymades.

Everlasting "silks" are historic looking and practical. *Photograph by Ken Kashian, courtesy David Davis Mansion.*

A wide variety of container shapes, sizes, and styles make it easy to decorate any surface in authentic style. *Photograph courtesy Winward International, Inc.*

Use as is or add a bow or streamer to ready-made wreaths. *Photograph courtesy Winward International, Inc.*

Striking arrangements like this one can be used singly on a console or as a pair on a mantel or long dining table. *Photograph courtesy Winward International, Inc.*

Tall pyramid shapes are very versatile. Flank a mantel with a pair. Tuck one inside a glass-fronted china cabinet. Place one atop a bookshelf. Options are endless. *Photographs courtesy Winward International, Inc.*

This appetizing arrangement is suitable for dining table, breakfast table or buffet. Use a pair on a large table. *Photographs courtesy Winward International, Inc.*

Tip: Care and keeping, and replacing faux botanicals

Historic style wreaths and swags save time and labor. Add ribbons and bows if you like. Switch colors of ribbons from year to year. *Photographs courtesy NDI.*

In the Victorian style, lace creates a romantic backdrop for a tabletop bouquet of faux fruit and greenery. *Photographs courtesy NDI.*

Ready-made arrangements include tabletop designs and Colonial-era kissing balls that were traditionally hung in doorways. *Photographs courtesy NDI.*

Decorative arrangements—often referred to as "silks"—may be thought of as "everlasting," but Kelly Billingsley of NDI says, "permanent doesn't mean forever." It does mean a long time. Sometimes called "botanicals" and made of silk fabric, these arrangements need TLC to look their best over time. Here are tips from Kelly:

- Do not place permanent botanicals and florals in direct sunlight. Like any item made of fabric, silk botanicals will fade.

- Do switch out arrangements from season to season—giving the arrangements and yourself a break.

- Do keep these arrangements clean (dust free). For easy cleaning, Kelly recommends NDI's trademark Newlife spray, which is just sprayed on. No wiping is necessary.

- Know when to retire an arrangement. Brand new historically-inspired arrangements create excitement that boosts morale—making bright spirits brighter.

More inspiring decorations with fruit used indoors and out can be seen in *Christmas at Historic Houses* and *Decorating for Christmas at Historic Homes*, McMillan and McMillan, Schiffer Publishing. All of these images encourage us to add our own unique touches to Christmas decorations using fruit—Nature's truly incredible works of art.

SOURCES

Photographers

JANEEN AGGEN, INDEPENDENCE TOURISM

14511 W. 81st St.
Lenexa, KS 66215
Tel: 913-599-2080
Email: janeena@sbcglobal.net

RUTH A.B. CLEGG/ANGELL FIRE ARTS

626 Ives Road
East Greenwich, RI 02818
Email: ruth@angellphoto.com

KEN KASHIAN, PHOTO SERVICES/ ILLINOIS FARM BUREAU

1701 Towanda Ave.
Bloomington, IL 61701
Email: kkashian@ilfb.org

BARBARA JUSTICE PHOTOGRAPHER

Tel: 210-573-2766
Email: barjus124@hotmail.com

Vendors of Materials Shown in Delicious Christmas Decorations

NDI

PO Box 847
Brewton, AL 36427
Tel: 800-522-2627
www.ndi.com

SAVE-ON-CRAFTS

www.saveoncrafts.com

WINWARD INTERNATIONAL, INC.

3089 Whipple Road
Union City, CA 94587
Tel: 800-888-8898, 510-886-6888
www.winwardsilks.com

Historic House Museums

See wonderful Christmas decorations with fruit at the historic house museums shown in this book, and a host of others listed here. Many have marvelous shops that make it so easy to bring a bit of traditional Christmas home. Visit these historic houses in *Christmas at Historic Houses* and *Decorating for Christmas at Historic Homes*, McMillan & McMillan, Schiffer Publishing and in person.

ADAMS HOUSE
22 Van Buren Street
Deadwood, South Dakota 57732
Tel: 605.578.3724
adamsmusuemandhouse.org

BALDWIN-REYNOLDS HOUSE
(PO Box 411)
639 Terrace Street
Meadville, PA 16335
Tel: 814.671.1030
jsherretts@baldwinreynolds.org

BARTOW-PELL MANSION MUSEUM
895 Shore Road, Pelham Bay Park
The Bronx, New York 10464
Tel: 718.885.1461
info@bpmm.org

BIDWELL HOUSE MUSEUM
100 Art School Road
PO Box 537
Monterey, MA 01245
Tel: 413.528.6888
bidwellhouse@gmail.com

BILLINGS FARM AND MUSEUM
5302 River Road, P.O. Box 489
Woodstock, Vermont 0509
Tel: 802.457.2335
www.billingsfarm.org

BILTMORE ESTATE
1 Approach Road
Asheville, North Carolina 28803
Tel: 800.624.1575 or 828-225-1333
www.biltmore.com

BINGHAM-WAGGONER HOME AND ESTATE
313 West Pacific
Independence, Missouri 64050
Tel: 816.461.3491
Fax: 816.461.1540
www.bwestate.org

BLITHEWOLD MANSION, GARDENS AND ARBORETUM
101 Ferry Road
Bristol, Rhode Island 02809
Tel: 401.253.2707
www.blithewold.org

BUTTERWORTH CENTER
1105-8th Street
Moline, Illinois 61265
Tel: 309.765.7970
www.butterworthcenter.com

CALVIN B. TAYLOR HOUSE MUSEUM
PO Box 351
208 North Main St.
Berlin, MD 21811
TaylorHouseMuseum@Verizon.net

CAMPBELL HOUSE MUSEUM
1508 Locust St.
St. Louis, MO 63103
Tel: 314.421.0325
campbellhm@earthlink.net

CAMPBELL HOUSE
2316 W. First Avenue
Spokane, WA 99204
Tel: 509.456.3931
themac@northwestmuseum.org

CHARLESTON MUSEUM
(Joseph Manigault House)
360 Meeting St.
Charleston, SC 29403
Tel: 843.722.2996, x 235
www.charlestonmuseum.org

CHIEF VANN HOUSE HISTORIC SITE
82 Georgia Highway 225 N
Chatsworth, Georgia 30705
Tel: 706.695.2598
www.gastateparks.org/info/chiefvann/

CHINQUA PENN PLANTATION
2138 Wentworth
Reidsville, NC 27320
Tel: 336.349.4576
lisa@chinquapenn.com

COLONIAL WILLIAMSBURG FOUNDATION
P. O. Box 1776
Williamsburg, VA 23187-1776
Tel: 757.229.1000
www.history.org/history

CROCKER HOUSE MUSEUM
15 Union Street
Mount Clemens, MI 48043
Tel: 586.465.2488,
Fax: 586.465.2932
crockerhousemuseum@sbcglobal.net

DAVID DAVIS MANSION
1000 E. Monroe Drive
Bloomington, Illinois 61701
Tel: 309.828,1084
Fax: 309.828.3493
davismansion@yahoo.com

DEERE-WIMAN HOUSE
817-11th Avenue
Moline, Illinois 61265
Tel: 309.765.7970
butterworthcenter.com

DRAYTON HALL
3380 Ashley River Road
Charleston, South Carolina 29414
Phone: 843.769.2600
www.draytonhall.org

EGYPT PLANTATION MUSEUM
(Heard-Northington House)
PO Box 219
Egypt, TX 77436-0219
egypt@wcnet.net
www.egypttexas.org

EMLEN PHYSICK ESTATE
1048 Washington Street
Cape May, New Jersey 08204
Tel: 800.275.4278 or 609.884-5404
Fax: 609.884.2006
Email: mac4arts@capemaymac.org
www.capemaymac.org

FLORENCE GRISWOLD MUSEUM

96 Lyme Street
Old Lyme, Connecticut 06371
Tel: 860.434.5542
www.flogris.org

GALLIER HOUSE (HERMANN-GRIMA & GALLIER HOUSES)

20 Saint Louis Street
New Orleans, LA 70112
el: 504.525.5661
Email: HGrimaGallier@aol.com
www.hgghh.org

HAZELWOOD HISTORIC HOUSE MUSEUM

1008 South Monroe Avenue
Greenbay, Wisconsin 54305
Tel: 920.437.1840
bchs@netnet.net
www.browncohistoricalsoc.org

HEARTHSIDE HOMESTEAD

677 Great Road
Lincoln, RI 02865
Tel: 401.726.0597
kathy.hartley@hearthsidehouse.org

HEARTHSTONE HISTORIC HOUSE MUSEUM

625 W. Prospect
Appleton, Wisconsin 54911
Tel: 920.730.8204
www.focol.org/hearthstone

HERMANN-GRIMA AND GALLIER HOUSES

20 Saint Louis Street
New Orleans, LA 70112
Tel: 504.525.5661
HGrimaGallier@aol.com
www.hgghh.org

JOEL LANE MUSEUM HOUSE

PO Box 10884
Raleigh, NC 27605 (US mail)
728 W. Hargett St.
Raleigh, NC 27603
Tel 919.833.3431
Fax: 919.833.9431
joellane@bellsouth.net

JOHN LIND HOME

622 Center Street
New Ulm, Minnesota 56073
Tel: 507.354.8802
lindhouse@newulmtel.net
www.lindhouse.org

JOSEPH MANIGAULT HOUSE

350 Meeting Street
Charleston, South Carolina
Phone: 843.722.2996
info@charlestonmuseum.org
www.charlestonmuseum.org

LYNDON BAINES JOHNSON RANCH

P.O. Box 329
Johnson City, TX 78636
Tel: 830.868.7128
www.nps.gov/lyjo/

LEU HOUSE MUSEUM

1920 N. Forest Avenue
Orlando, FL 32803-1537
Tel: 407.246.2620
Fax 407.246.2849
rbowden@cityoforlando.net
www.leugardens.org

JAIL, MARSHAL'S HOME AND MUSEUM

217 North Main Street
Independence, Missouri 64050
Tel: 816.252.1892
www.jchs.org

MARJORIE KINNAN RAWLINGS FARM

18700 South CR 325
Cross Creek, Florida 32640
Tel: 352.466.3672
www.marojiekinnanrawlings.org

MAYMONT MANSION

1700 Hampton St.
Richmond, VA 23220
Tel: 804.358.7166, x 329
info@maymont.org
www.maymont.org

MOLLY BROWN HOUSE MUSEUM

1340 Pennsylvania Street
Denver, Colorado 80203
Fax: 303.832.4092
Tel: 303.832.2340
www.mollybrown.org

MONTICELLO

P.O. Box 316
Charlottesville, Virginia 22902
Tel: 434.984.9822
www.monticello.org

MORRIS BUTLER HOUSE

1204 North Park Avenue
Indianapolis, Indiana 46202
Tel: 317.636.5409
Fax: 317.636.2630
Email: mbhouse@historiclandmarks.org
www.historiclandmarks.org

MOUNT CLARE

Carroll Park
1500 Washington Blvd
Baltimore, Maryland 21230
Tel: 410.837.3262
www.montclare.org

MOUNT VERNON

Mount Vernon Ladies' Association
PO Box 110
Mount Vernon, VA 22121
Tel: 703.780.2000
www.mountvernon.org

MY OLD KENTUCKY HOME

Federal Hill
501 East Stephen Foster Avenue
Bardstown, Kentucky 40004-0323
Tel: 502.348.3502
MyOldKentuckyHome@ky.gov
www.parks.ky.gov/stateparks/mk/

OLDFIELDS–LILLY HOUSE AND GARDENS

4000 Michigan Road
Indianapolis, Indiana 46208-3326
Tel: 317.923.1331
www.ima-art.org

PETERSEN HOUSE MUSEUM

1414 W. Southern Avenue
Tempe, AZ 85282
www.tempe.gov/petersenhouse/

PETTENGILL-MORRON HOUSE

1212 W. Moss Avenue
Peoria, IL 61606
Tel: 309.674.1921
Fax 309.674.1882
www.peoriahistoricalsociety.org

PHYSICK HOUSE
(Emlen Physick Estate)
1048 Washington Street
Cape May, New Jersey 08204
Tel:: 800.275.4278 or 609.884-5404
Fax: 609.884.2006
mac4arts@capemaymac.org
www.capemaymac.org

PITTOCK MANSION
3229 NW Pittock Drive
Portland, Oregon 97210
Tel: 503.823.3624
www.pittockmansion.com

RICHARDS-DAR HOUSE MUSEUM
256 North Joachim Street
Mobile, AL 36603
Tel: 251.208.7320
2638smbg@bellsouth.net
www.richardsdarhouse.com

RIVERSDALE HOUSE MUSEUM
4811 Riversdale Road
Riverdale Park, MD 20737
Tel: 301.864.0420
Ann.wass@pgparks.com
www.pgparks.com

ROSELAND COTTAGE (BOWEN HOUSE)
556 Rte. 169,
Woodstock, CT
www.historicnewengland.org/historic-properties/homes/roseland-cottage/roseland-cottage

SAMUEL CUPPLES HOUSE AT ST. LOUIS UNIVERSITY
3673 West Pine Mall
St. Louis, MO 63108
Tel 314.977.3575
Fax 314.977.3581
www.slu.edu/x27031.xml

THE SHERWOOD-DAVIDSON HOUSE MUSEUM
Veterans' Park
PO Box 785
Newark, OH 43058-0785
Tel: 740.345.4898
sherwooddavidson@yahoo.co
www.lchs@alink.com

SLIFER HOUSE MUSEUM
80 Magnolia Drive
Lewisburg, PA 17837
Tel: 570.524.2245
Gary.parks@albrightcare.org
www.albrightcare.org/slifer-house

TUDOR PLACE HISTORIC HOUSE AND GARDEN
1644 31st Street NW
Washington, DC 20007
Tel: 202.965.0400
Fax: 202.965.0164
info@tudorplace.org
www.tudorplace.org

VAILE MANSION - DE WITT MUSEUM
1500 North Liberty
Independence, Missouri 64050
Tel: 816 325-7430
www.vailemansion.org

VAN CORTLANDT MANOR

525 South Riverside Avenue
Croton-on-Hudson, NY 10520
Tel: 914.271.8981
Email: info@hudsonvalley.org
www.hudsonvalley.org

WADDESDON MANOR

Nr Aylesbury
Buckinghamshire
HP18 OJH
United Kingdom
Tel: +44(0) 1296 658586
Fax: +44(0) 1296 653212
waddesdonmanor@nationaltrust.org.uk
www.waddesdon.org.uk

WADE HOUSE

W7824 Center Street
PO Box 34
Greenbush, WI 33026
Tel 920.526.3271
Fax? 920.526.3626
David.simmons@wisconsinhistory.org
www.wadehouse.org

WEBB-DEANE-STEVENS MUSEUM

211 Main St.
Wethersfield, CT 06109
Tel: 860-529-0612, x14
clyle@webb-deane-stevens.org
www.webb-deane-stevens.org

WHITE HOUSE
1600 Pennsylvania Avenue
Washington, D.C. 20500
Tel: 202.456.7041
White House Visitor Center, Southeast corner of 15th and E Streets
www.whitehouse.gov

WHITEHALL
Henry Morrison Flagler Museum
One Whitehall Way
P.O. Box 969
Palm Beach, Florida 33480
Tel: 561.655.2833
www.flaglermuseum.us